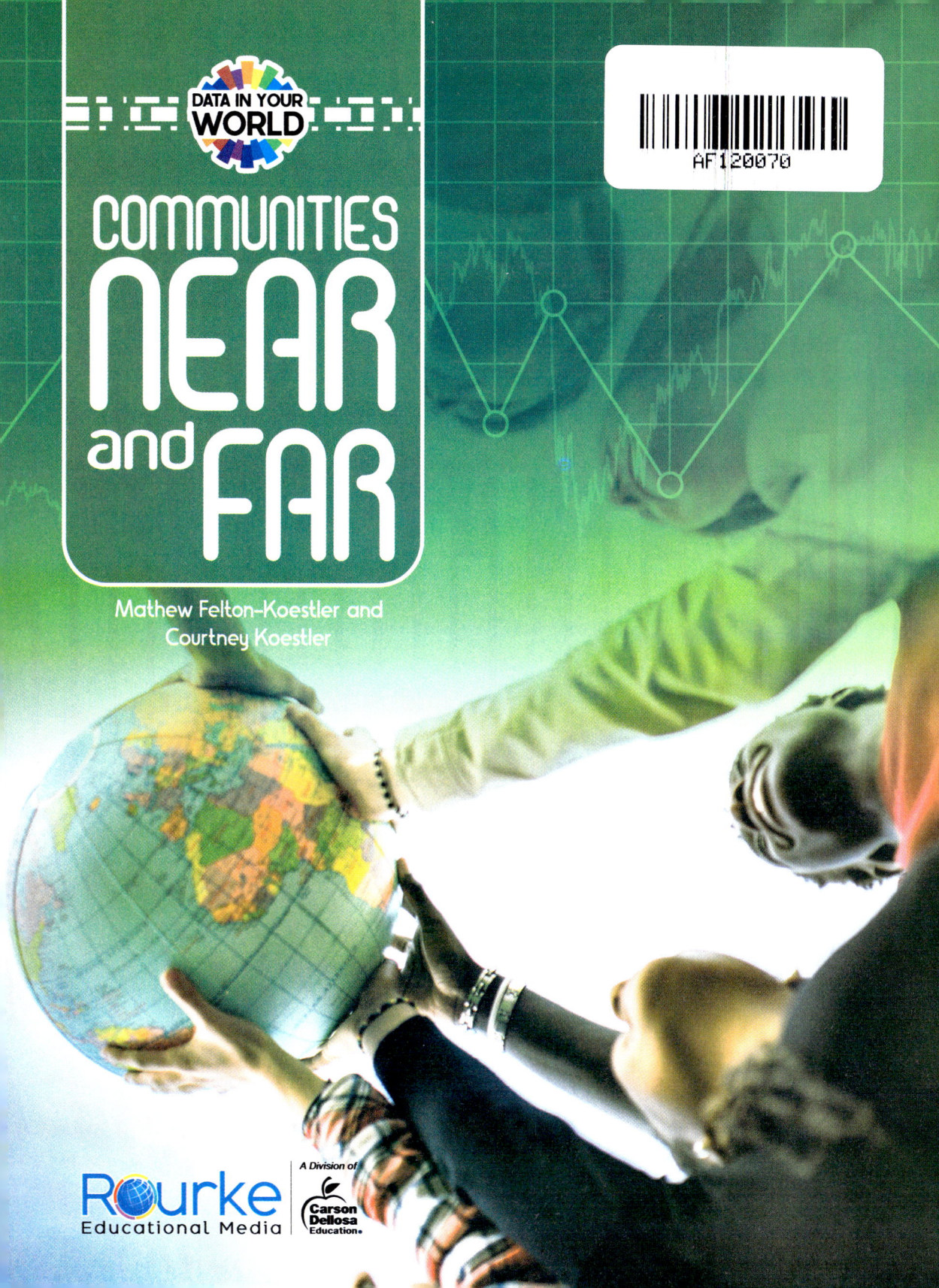

ROURKE'S SCHOOL to HOME CONNECTIONS
BEFORE AND DURING READING ACTIVITIES

Before Reading: *Building Background Knowledge and Vocabulary*

Building background knowledge can help children process new information and build upon what they already know. Before reading a book, it is important to tap into what children already know about the topic. This will help them develop their vocabulary and increase their reading comprehension.

Questions and Activities to Build Background Knowledge:

1. Look at the front cover of the book and read the title. What do you think this book will be about?
2. What do you already know about this topic?
3. Take a book walk and skim the pages. Look at the table of contents, photographs, captions, and bold words. Did these text features give you any information or predictions about what you will read in this book?

Vocabulary: *Vocabulary Is Key to Reading Comprehension*

Use the following directions to prompt a conversation about each word.

- Read the vocabulary words.
- What comes to mind when you see each word?
- What do you think each word means?

Vocabulary Words:
- community
- diversity
- ethnicity
- Indian reservations
- mortgage
- population
- race
- redlining
- segregation
- social scientists
- territories
- variation

During Reading: *Reading for Meaning and Understanding*

To achieve deep comprehension of a book, children are encouraged to use close reading strategies. During reading, it is important to have children stop and make connections. These connections result in deeper analysis and understanding of a book.

 ### Close Reading a Text

During reading, have children stop and talk about the following:

- Any confusing parts
- Any unknown words
- Text to text, text to self, text to world connections
- The main idea in each chapter or heading

Encourage children to use context clues to determine the meaning of any unknown words. These strategies will help children learn to analyze the text more thoroughly as they read.

When you are finished reading this book, turn to pages 44 and 45 for **Questions for Reflection** and an **Extension Activity**.

Table of Contents

The Importance of Data 4

Our Global Community 6

Our National Community 10

Racial Diversity in the United States 12

Understanding Race and Ethnicity 14

Our State Community 22

Our City and Neighborhood Communities 28

Getting Involved 42

Questions for Reflection 44

Extension Activity 45

Glossary 46

Index 47

Bibliography 47

About the Authors 48

The Importance of Data

Data can help us understand the world, our country, and our local communities. It can be a valuable tool for understanding who we are as a society, what makes our communities the same or different, and how communities near and far are changing over time. Data can also show where inequalities exist in our society so that we know where change is needed.

Have you ever answered a survey or been interviewed about your opinion on something? Have you ever participated in an experiment? Your input was valuable data. Mathematicians and **social scientists** collect data in a variety of ways, including surveys, polls, interviews, experiments, observations, and more.

Is Data Singular or Plural?

Over the years, scientists have treated the word *data* as plural, and they would write "These data show that ..." However, today, it's increasingly common to treat *data* as singular, such as "This data shows that ..." which is what we will do in this book.

Our Global Community

No matter where you live in the world, you are part of the same global **community** as everyone else. Every nation on every continent is closely connected by modern telecommunications, like the internet and email. All 7.8 billion people in the world are connected economically, socially, and politically.

In 1968, the world **population** growth rate was at a high of 2.09%. This means that for every 100 people, there were about two more people the following year. But it's been declining ever since. In 2020, the growth rate was 1.05%. By 2100, it is projected to be close to 0%, meaning the total number of people will not increase or decrease. What do you think might be a reason for this decline?

Look at the bar graph on the next page. It shows the ten countries with the largest populations in 2020. What do you notice? What do you wonder? What questions do you have?

? Think about these questions as you look at the bar graph:

- What does the height of each bar indicate?
- Would you and the people you know be shown on this graph? If so, where?
- Which country has the largest population?
- How does the United States compare to other countries?
- Can you find these countries on a map?

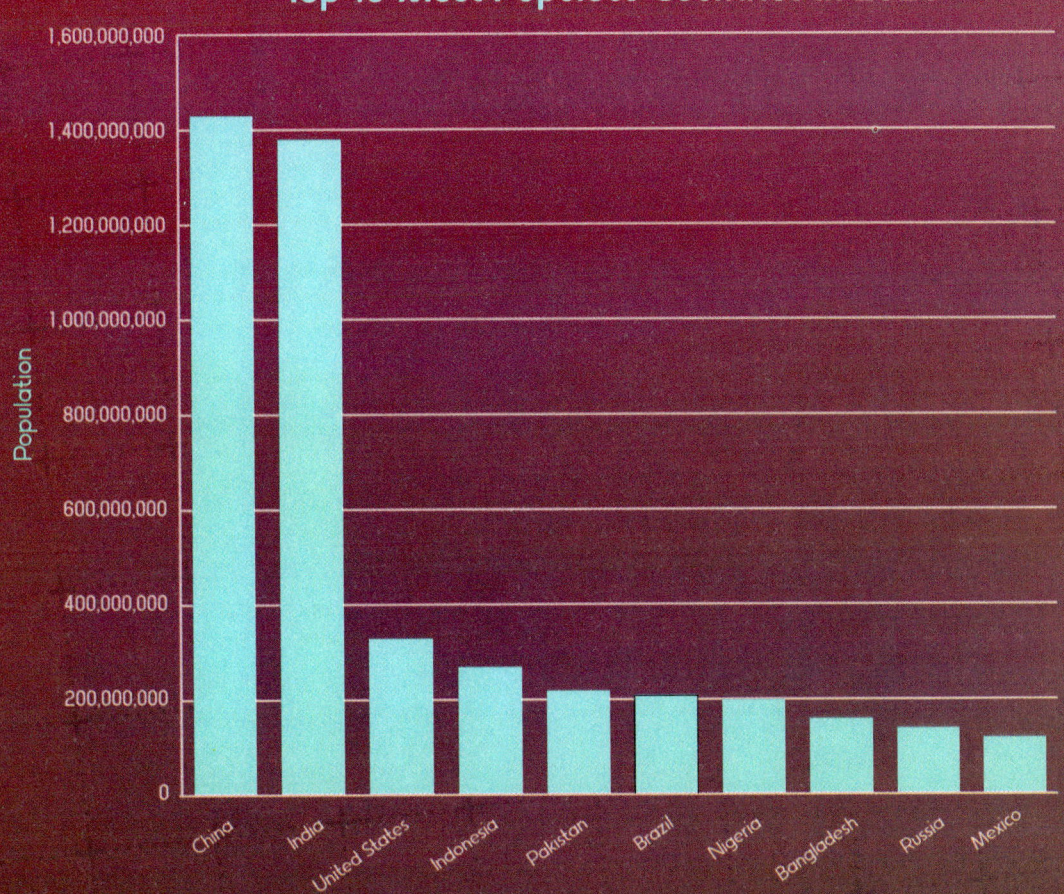

Our National Community

Another community we belong to is our country, the United States. When most people talk about the United States, they often focus on the 50 states. But the U.S. also includes Washington D.C. (a district, not a state), five inhabited U.S. **territories**, and 326 **Indian reservations**.

Using Specific Terms or Tribal Names

The terms *American Indian*, *Indian*, *Native American*, *Native*, and *Indigenous American* are all commonly used to describe the people native to the Americas. Many people in these groups prefer to be called by their specific tribal name, like the Little River Band of Ottawa Indians, or have preferences about specific terms.

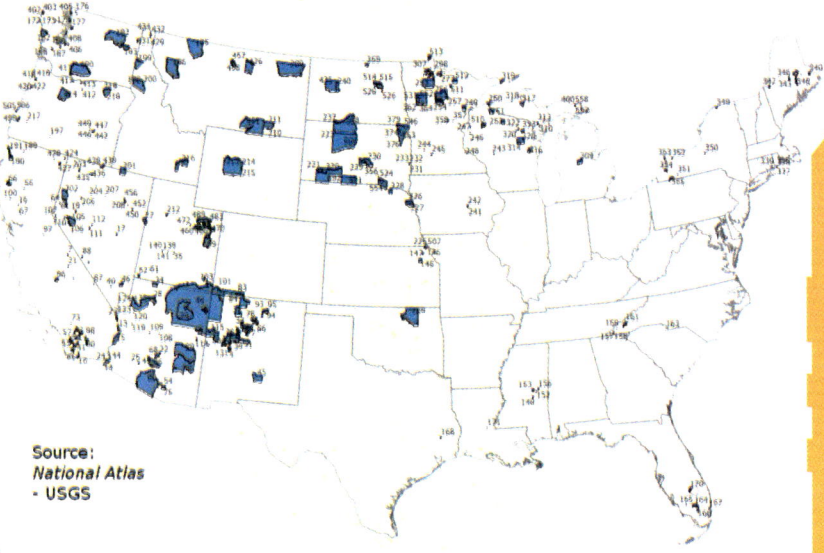

Over 50 Million Acres of American Indian Heritage

This map shows all of the American Indian reservations in the continental U.S. (does not include Alaska and Hawaii). These reservations cover a total of 56,200,000 acres of land!

Part of the U.S., but with Exceptions

The U.S. territories are part of the U.S., but they are not classified as states. Even though they are not represented in the U.S. Congress and residents can't vote in U.S. elections, each inhabited territory has its own unique history, geography, and experiences for residents and visitors.

Racial Diversity in the United States

Think about these questions as you look at the chart:

- What does each section of the pie chart represent?
- Why do you think "Hispanic" is not included in "Race"?
- Think about yourself, your friends, and your family. Would they be represented in this chart? Why or why not?

Where are you on this pie chart? Where would your neighborhood be represented on this pie chart?

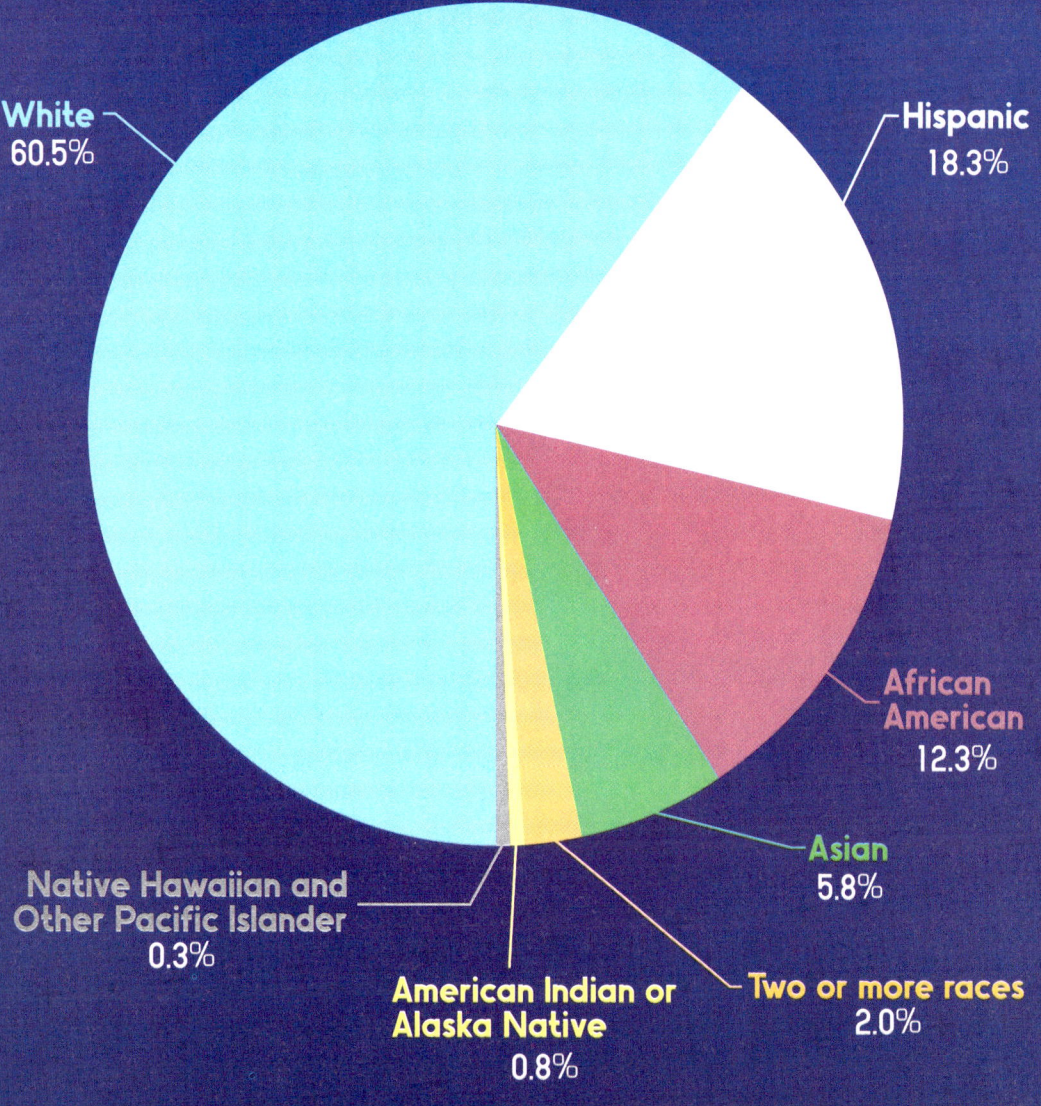

Race and Hispanic Origin in the U.S. (2018)

- White 60.5%
- Hispanic 18.3%
- African American 12.3%
- Asian 5.8%
- Two or more races 2.0%
- American Indian or Alaska Native 0.8%
- Native Hawaiian and Other Pacific Islander 0.3%

The term *Hispanic* refers to **ethnicity**, not **race**. Ethnicity is about cultural connections, while race sometimes describes physical traits (like skin color) or different social identities.

Understanding Race and Ethnicity

Race and **ethnicity** are complex ideas, and people think about them in many ways. Sometimes the ways people think about themselves do not line up with how the government collects data about them. For example, our graphs use the term *Hispanic*, which mainly refers to whether someone (or their ancestors) speaks Spanish or identifies with Spanish culture. However, people in this group may use other terms that connect with their geographical or cultural ties, like *Mexican American*, *Colombian*, or more broadly as *Latino*.

Gender and Grammar

In Spanish, words are grammatically gendered, like *Latino* and *Latina*. The terms *Latinx* or *Latine* can be used as gender-inclusive terms for people who don't identify as female or male. In this book, we use *Latino* because this is what government agencies typically use.

Some people identify as both Black and Hispanic or White and Hispanic. Different data sources count these people differently. Some data sources count these people in both categories (under Black and Hispanic). Other data sources (like the data sources used for this book) only include them under the category of Hispanic.

Frequently Used Terms for Racial & Ethnic Groups by the U.S. Government in 2021

- American Indian or Alaska Native
- Asian
- Black or African American
- Hispanic or Latino
- Pacific Islander
- White
- More than one race

Perhaps most importantly, the way we view and understand race and ethnicity has more to do with our thinking than it does with a scientific method of categorizing people. Like our society, the language we use to discuss race and ethnicity is always evolving.

The Changing Categories of Ethnic Groups in the U.S.

The terms the government uses to define people have changed multiple times over the years, and will probably continue to change for years to come. For example, Hawaiian, Part Hawaiian, Samoan, and Guamanian used to fall under the Asian category on a census form. Now they have their own category: Pacific Islander.

Data can be used to show how populations are changing. Look at the clustered bar graph on the next page. It shows how the racial/ethnic makeup of the U.S. changed from 2003 to 2018. What do you notice? What do you wonder? What questions do you have?

? Think about these questions as you look at the bar graph:

- What do the two colors represent?
- What does the height of each bar mean?
- Can you tell how many students of each race there were in 2003 and 2018, and will be in 2029?
- Think about yourself, your friends, and other students you know. Would they be represented in this graph? Why or why not?

Race/Ethnicity in the U.S. (2003 vs 2018)

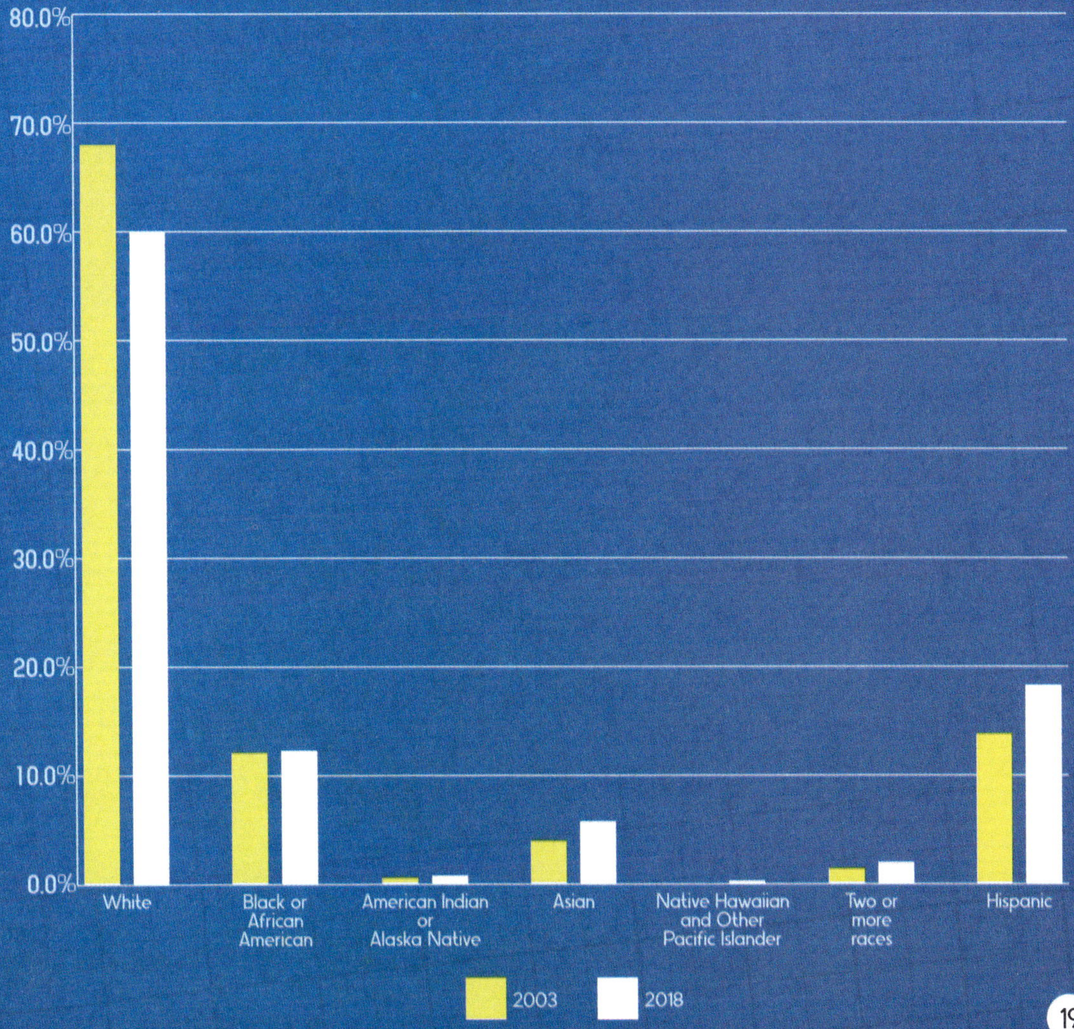

Race	2003	2018
White	~68%	~60%
Black or African American	~12%	~12.5%
American Indian or Alaska Native	~0.8%	~1%
Asian	~4.5%	~6%
Native Hawaiian and Other Pacific Islander	~0.2%	~0.3%
Two or more races	~1.5%	~2.5%
Hispanic	~14%	~18.5%

The two colors show the percentages for each race/ethnicity in 2003 (yellow) compared with 2018 (white). In the U.S., the percentage of White people has decreased, while the percentage of people of color has increased. Social scientists expect this trend to continue and predict that White people will be less than half of the U.S. population around 2045.

If you think that the population trend shown in this graph will mean more **diversity** in the U.S. in the future, you're right! Can you think of some benefits to having a more diverse country to live in? How would more diversity affect your life?

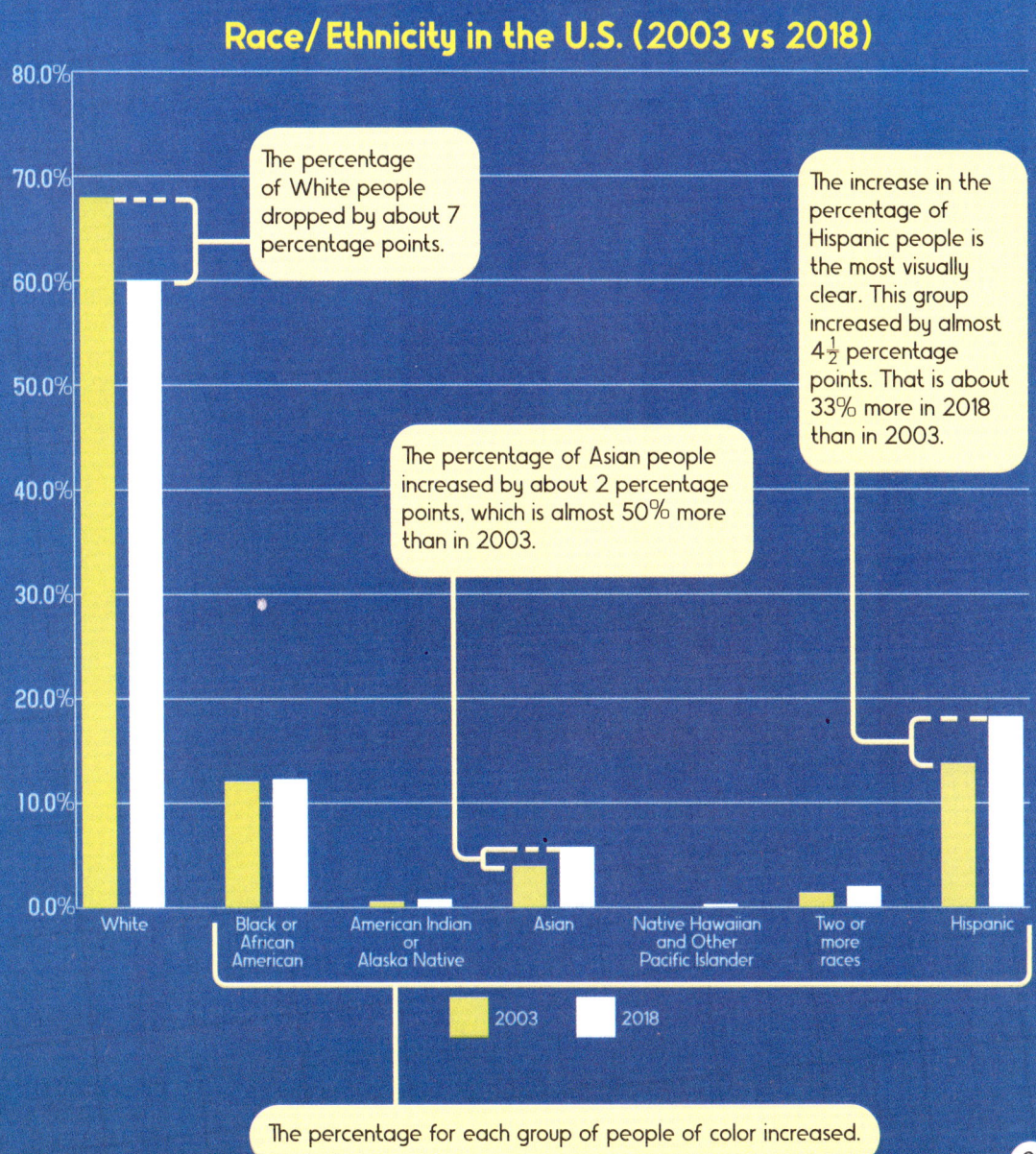

Our State Community

Think about your city or state. What do you want to learn about it? We can use large data sets to understand what's happening in the world or in our country. To focus on our city or state, we can use more focused data sets.

It's important to know that all data has **variation** within it. For example, just because about 60% of the U.S. population is White does not mean that 60% of every neighborhood, city, or state is White. Data can help us see how overall trends (like for the whole country) compare to more specific trends (like for a state or city).

Think about the state you live in. Is it as diverse as the United States as a whole? Is it less diverse? What would the data on diversity look like for your state?

Look at the table about the most (California) and least (Wyoming) populated states, as well as the U.S. as a whole. What do you notice? What do you wonder? What questions do you have?

Think about these questions as you look at the table:

- How does Wyoming's population compare to California's population?
- What is the same about Wyoming, California, and the whole U.S.? What is different? Why do you think this is?
- How does the table show the same information as the pie chart on page 13, but in a different way?

Population and Race/Ethnicity Data from 2018

	Wyoming	California	U.S.
Population	578,759	39,512,223	328,239,523
Children and Adults			
Children (under 18)	23%	23%	23%
Adults	77%	77%	77%
Race and Ethnicity			
White	83%	38%	60.5%
Black	1.1%	5%	12.3%
American Indian or Alaska Native	4%	0.6%	0.8%
Asian	0.9%	15%	5.8%
Native Hawaiian and Other Pacific Islander	0.2%	0.6%	0.3%
Two or more Races	1.8%	1.9%	2%
Hispanic	9%	39%	18.3%

Did you notice that California's population is much larger than Wyoming's? It's about 68 times larger! What did you notice about California's diversity? If you saw that it has a much smaller percentage of White people and a much larger percentage of both Asian and Hispanic, or Latino, people, you are right!

Is the difference in population or diversity of these two states surprising to you? Why or why not?

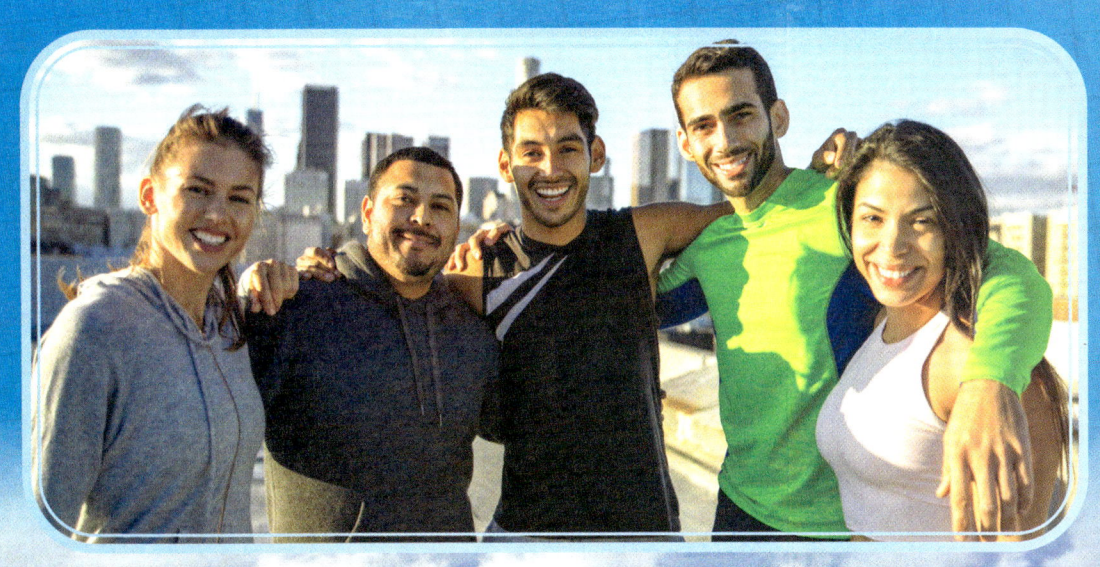

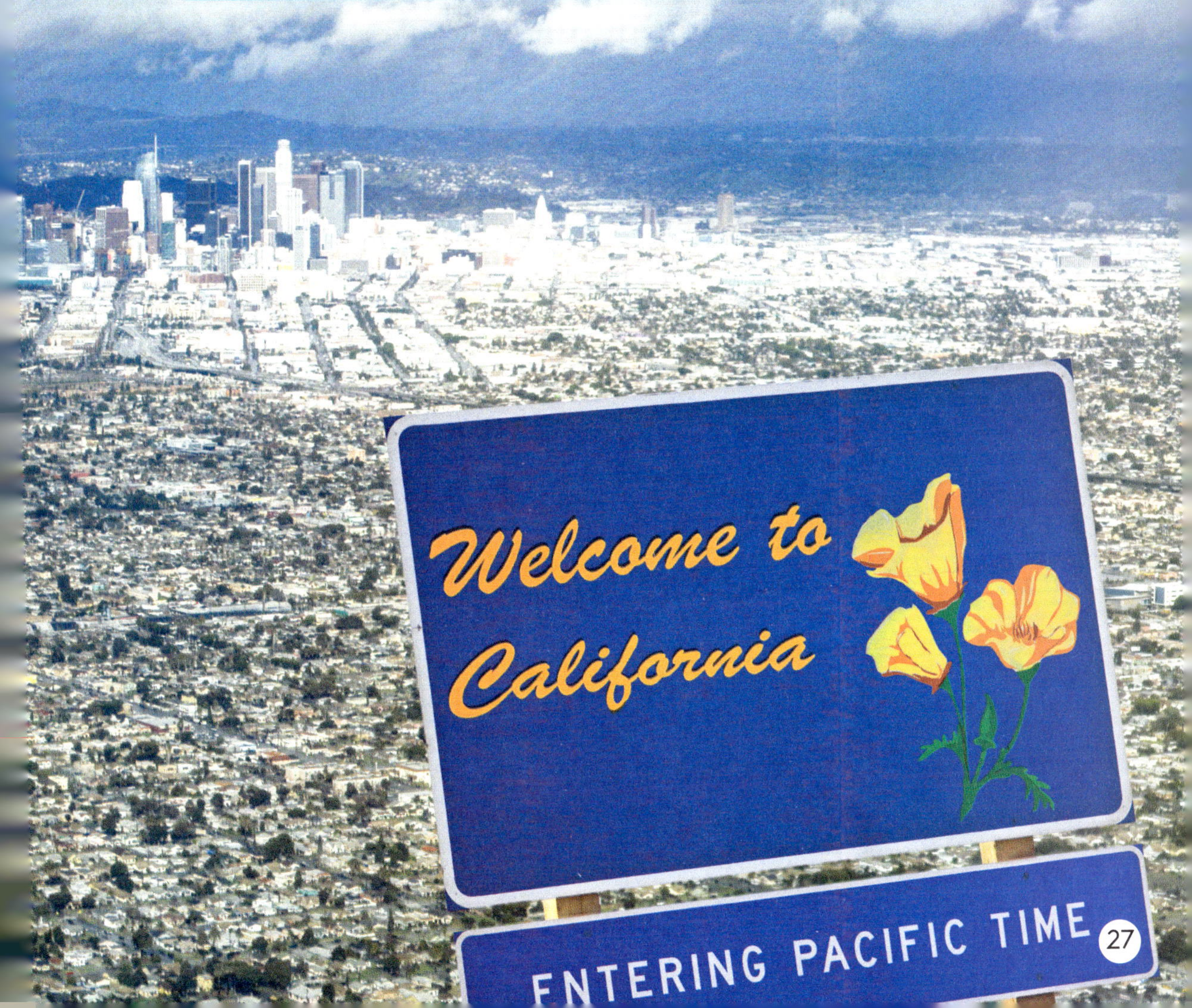
Welcome to
California
ENTERING PACIFIC TIME

Our City and Neighborhood Communities

When you look around your city or neighborhood, do you see a lot of diversity? Do you have neighbors of different racial or ethnic groups than yours? Or do most people look like you?

In the U.S., some areas in cities and states are **segregated**. In these areas you will see mostly people who share the same race or ethnicity.

Segregation at the Miami Orange Bowl football game on January 2, 1956

For topics that connect data to geography, a map like the one on the next page is a good tool to use. This map shows different colored dots for each person of a different race or ethnicity who lives in Washington D.C., our nation's capital. The dashed lines show the borders of the city.

Look at the map. What do you notice? What do you wonder? What questions do you have?

❓ Think about these questions as you look at the dot map:

- What do you think the dark areas represent?
- What patterns do you notice? Why do you think these patterns exist?

Small Dots with Big Meaning

In this dot map, each dot shows a person of a specific race or ethnicity. Dot maps help us see the relationship between data and geography. These maps can show many things, like patterns in infectious diseases, earthquakes, insect migration, and more.

Did you notice that many Black people live in the southeast section of the city? Did you also notice that many White people live on the western side of the city? There are also a few neighborhoods in the north and west where many Hispanic people live. Why do you think there are clusters of racial or ethnic groups? Does this information surprise you?

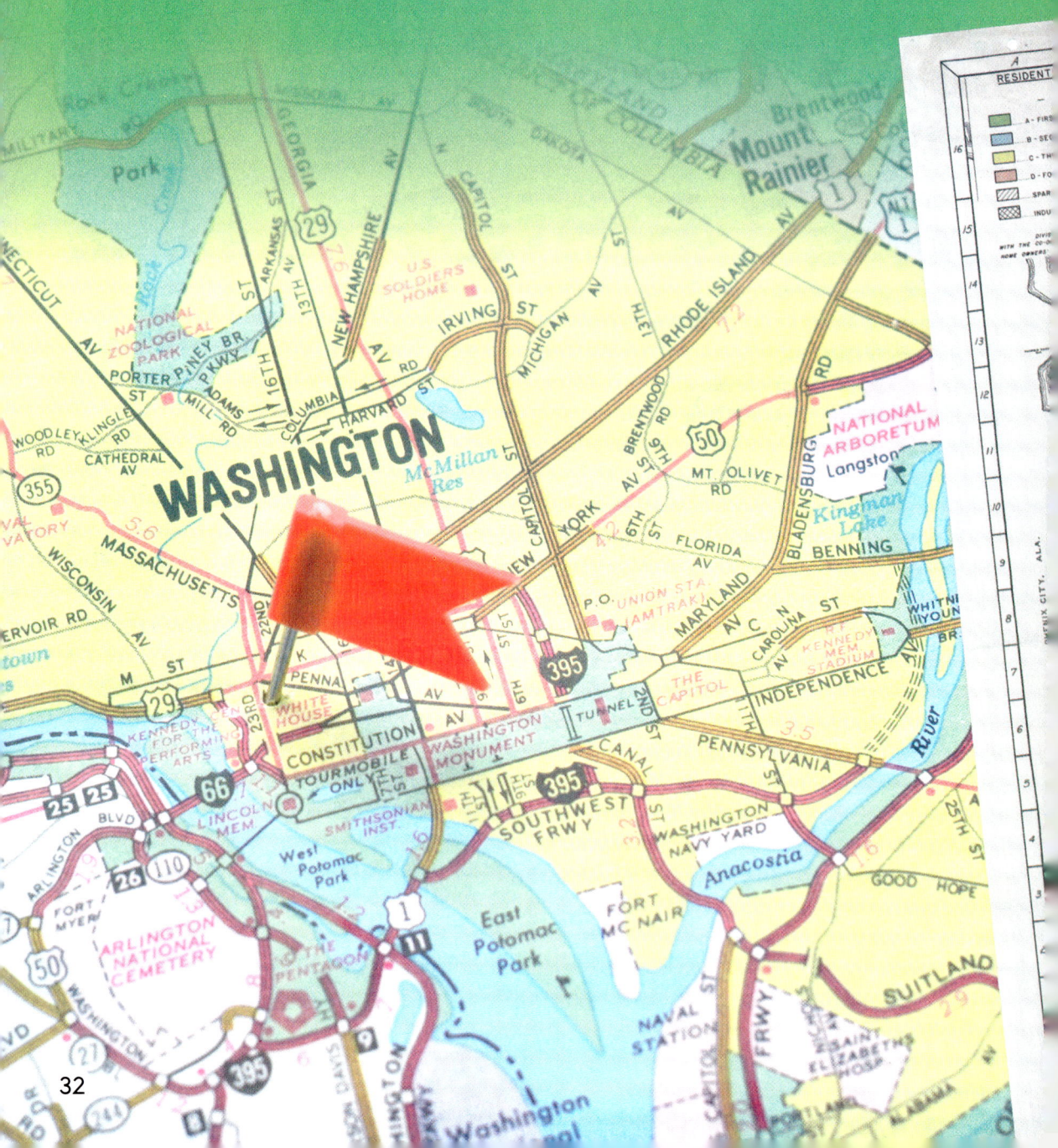

Communities can be segregated for a variety of reasons, including cost of living, discrimination, and even people's preferences. But one significant factor almost 100 years ago that led to **segregation** in the U.S. was the discriminatory practice of **redlining**.

Seeing Red

In redlining, the government outlined mostly Black neighborhoods in red ink on maps as a warning to banks to not lend money to them.

In the 1930s, the government created maps of neighborhoods based on the racial/ethnic makeup of the areas. Green areas were "best," blue were "still desirable," yellow were "definitely declining," and red were "hazardous." The government considered the red neighborhoods undesirable because they were made up of mostly Black people, but also Catholics, Jews, and immigrants.

The maps were used by banks to determine who they should—and should not—give loans and **mortgages** to. This was not good for people in red areas. Redlining made the dream of homeownership impossible for them.

How does learning about redlining make you feel? How do you think the victims of redlining felt? What do you think are the lasting effects of redlining?

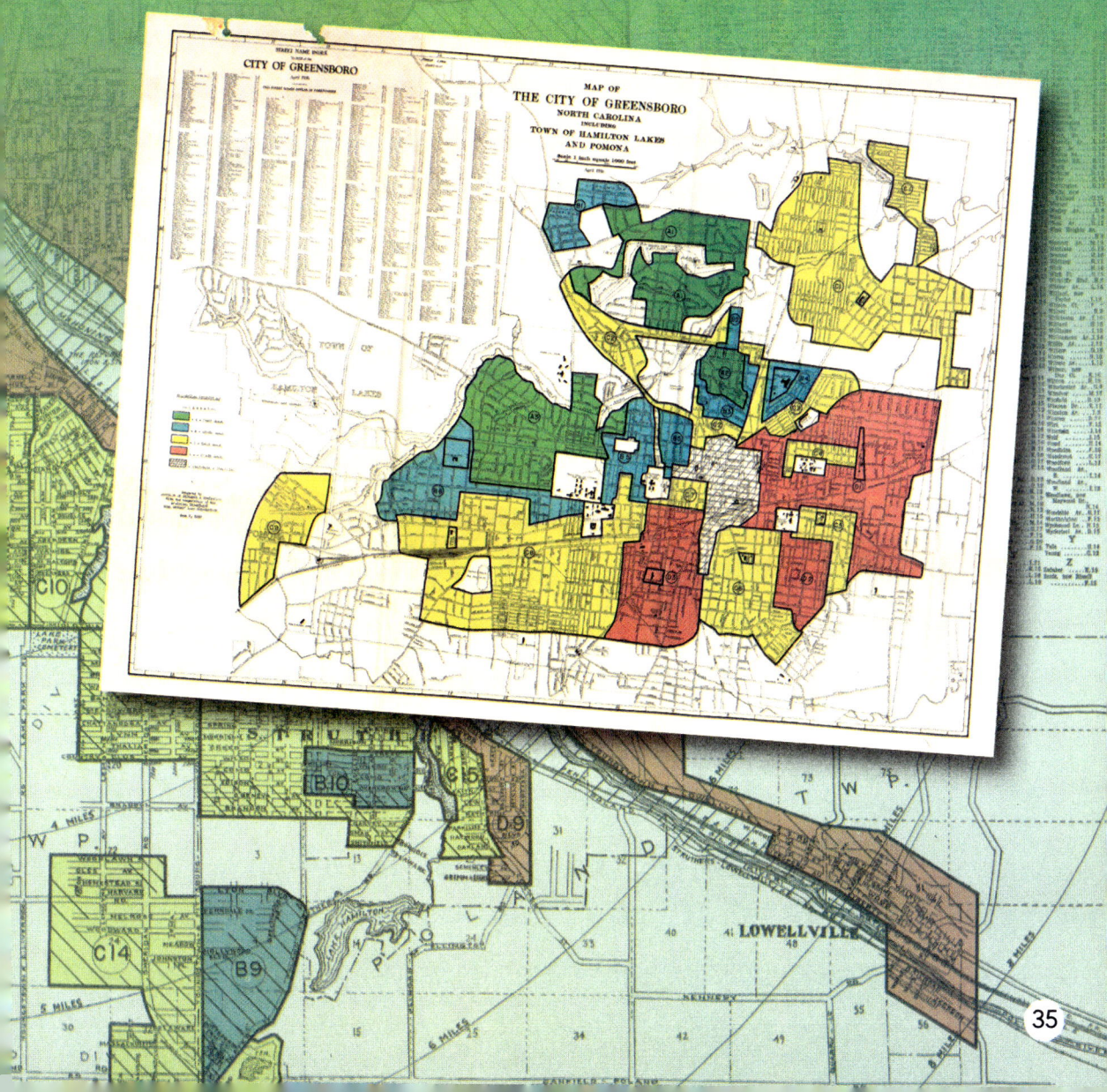

Even though people who lived in redlined areas were just as likely to pay their mortgages as people who lived in the other areas, banks and the government were not likely to give them mortgages, or they made the mortgages too expensive. This made it very difficult for families in those communities to buy homes.

This lack of homeownership led to neighborhoods that became dilapidated, or rundown. Many businesses left these neighborhoods because of this. Schools in these areas suffered, too. Without tax money from homeowners or businesses, schools didn't have much money for expenses.

Effects of Redlining on Schools

Schools are funded partly by money that homeowners and businesses pay in their property taxes. An area with homes and businesses will have more money to put toward schools than an area with rundown properties or no businesses. Money for schools is used to pay teachers' salaries, buy supplies and technology, maintain buildings and playgrounds, and more. This is one reason why many people think we should fund schools differently in the U.S.

In 1968, the Fair Housing Act law was passed, which made redlining illegal. It became illegal to refuse to sell or rent a home or apartment to people based on their race, color, religion, or the country they were from. It was also illegal to discriminate against people with disabilities, against families with children, or based on someone's sex, gender identity, or sexual orientation.

Signing Day

The House of Representatives passed the Fair Housing Act on April 10, 1968, and President Lyndon B. Johnson signed it into law the next day.

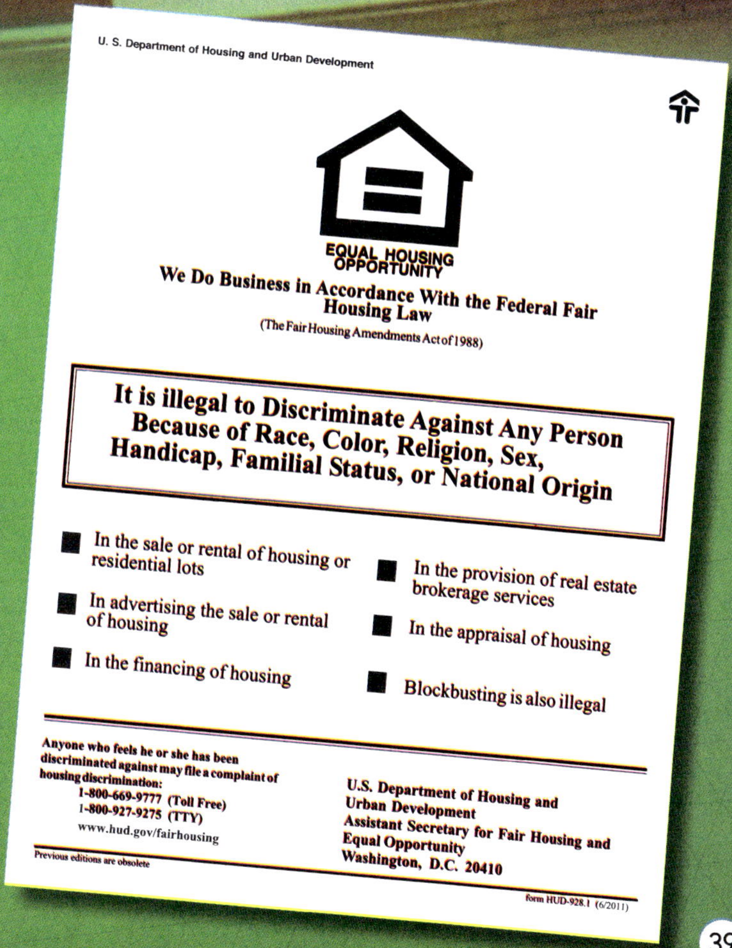

U. S. Department of Housing and Urban Development

EQUAL HOUSING OPPORTUNITY

We Do Business in Accordance With the Federal Fair Housing Law

(The Fair Housing Amendments Act of 1988)

It is illegal to Discriminate Against Any Person Because of Race, Color, Religion, Sex, Handicap, Familial Status, or National Origin

- In the sale or rental of housing or residential lots
- In advertising the sale or rental of housing
- In the financing of housing
- In the provision of real estate brokerage services
- In the appraisal of housing
- Blockbusting is also illegal

Anyone who feels he or she has been discriminated against may file a complaint of housing discrimination:
1-800-669-9777 (Toll Free)
1-800-927-9275 (TTY)
www.hud.gov/fairhousing

U.S. Department of Housing and Urban Development
Assistant Secretary for Fair Housing and Equal Opportunity
Washington, D.C. 20410

Previous editions are obsolete

form HUD-928.1 (6/2011)

Unfortunately, the negative effects of redlining can still be seen today. Communities targeted by redlining years ago have not been able to build generational wealth, or assets passed from one generation to the next, such as real estate. Many continue to struggle financially today. People of color are still much less likely to own their home today compared to White people.

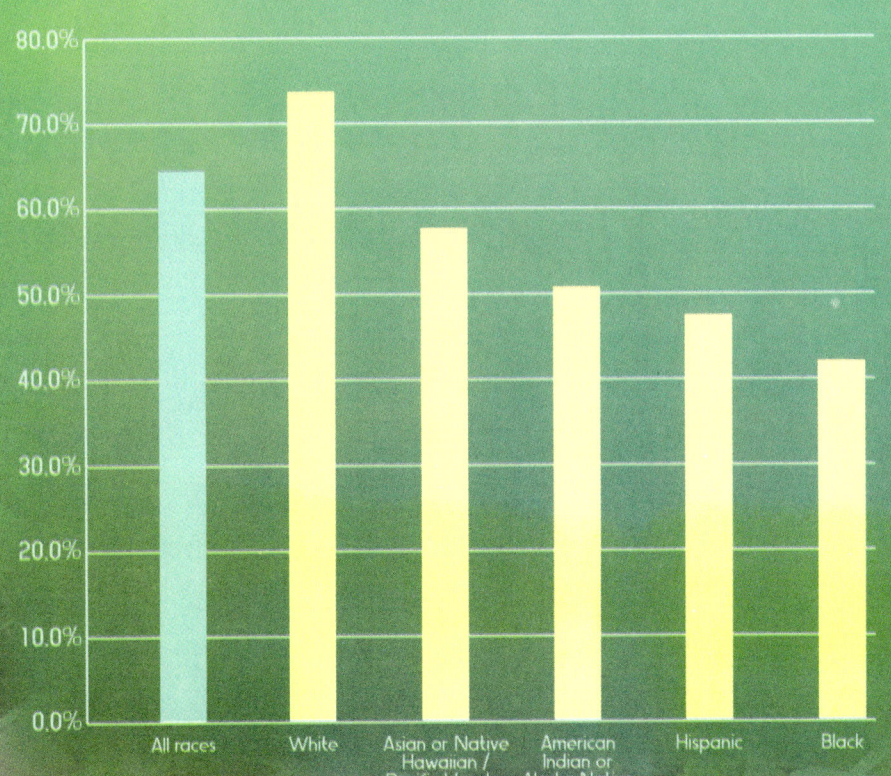

Homeownership Rates in 2019:

All races: 64.6%

White: 73.3%

Asian or Native Hawaiian / Pacific Islander: 57.7%

American Indian or Alaska Native: 50.8%

Hispanic: 47.5%

Black: 42.1%

Getting Involved

Throughout history, people have worked to fight injustices in their communities near and far. Even children have taken action! Marley Dias, an 11-year-old girl living in New Jersey, was frustrated with books always having White boys as the main characters. So she started the #1000BlackGirlBooks campaign to collect 1,000 books to donate that featured Black girls or women as main characters. She collected over 11,000 books to donate to schools around the world, and now she is a teenage social activist and writer doing good throughout the world.

As a member of your neighborhood or community, what is something that you notice and wonder about that you would like to change? Do you see areas for improvement? How could you use data to learn about and support your cause?

Questions for Reflection

Let's connect data to your life. Answer the following questions and record your answers in a notebook.

1. How do you and your family use data in your everyday life?

2. What is some data you could collect about your city or community? Your state? The country? The world?

3. What changes do you see in the world around you? How can you use data to understand these changes?

4. What inequalities do you see in your world, and how could data help you better understand them?

5. What can you do to challenge the inequalities that you see?

Extension Activity

Informed citizens learn how to find, analyze, and discuss data about our world. Now it's your turn to find and analyze data on a topic that interests you.

1. Choose a topic about your community, your state, your country, or the world that you want to know more about.

2. See what data and graphs you can find about your topic in news articles or on the internet.

    a. Find out more about your community or the United States here: https://www.census.gov/data/data-tools/quickfacts.html

    b. You can do more advanced searches here: https://www.census.gov/programs-surveys/cps/data/data-tools.html

    c. You can explore the Racial Dot Map project, which shows racial segregation in neighborhoods, here: https://demographics.coopercenter.org/racial-dot-map

    d. You can learn more about redlining here: https://dsl.richmond.edu/panorama/redlining/

3. Find one or more graphs about your topic and analyze what they are showing you.

    a. Can you explain the data the graph shows?

    b. What comparisons can you make within each graph? How can you compare the graphs?

    c. What does this mean for the real world?

4. Share what you found with a friend or an adult. Ask each other questions about the graph(s) and what they mean.

Glossary

community (kuh-MYOO-ni-tee): a group of people or nations having a common history or common social, economic, or political interests; people with common interests living in a particular area

diversity (di-VUR-si-tee): the inclusion of people of different races or cultures

ethnicity (eth-NI-si-tee): a particular ethnic affiliation or group

Indian reservation (IN-dee-uhn rez-ur-VAY-shuhn): public land set aside for American Indians

mortgage (MOR-gij): a type of loan used to finance a property

population (pahp-yuh-LAY-shuhn): all the individuals occupying an area

race (rase): a group that humans are divided into based on physical traits

redlining (RED-line-ing): to withhold loans or mortgages from neighborhoods considered poor economic risks

segregation (seg-ri-GAY-shuhn): the separation or isolation of a race, class, or ethnic group

social scientist (SOH-shuhl SYE-uhn-tist): a scientist who studies the link between society and human behavior

territories (TER-i-tor-eez): a part of the U.S. not included within any state but organized with a separate legislature; residents are U.S. citizens

variation (VAIR-ee-ay-shuhn): a measure of the change in data

Index

discrimination 33, 38, 39

Fair Housing Act 38, 39

graph 8, 9, 14, 18, 19, 21

homeownership 35, 37, 40

illegal 38, 39

injustice 42

loan 35, 36

Marley Dias 42

population 8, 9, 18, 20, 21, 23, 24–26

property tax(es) 37

redlining 33, 35, 36, 38, 40, 45

trend 20, 21, 23

Bibliography

"Homeownership rates show that Black Americans are currently the least likely group to own homes." www.usafacts.org/articles/homeownership-rates-by-race. (accessed September 15, 2021).

United Nations Department of Economic and Social Affairs. "World Population Prospects 2019." https://population.un.org/wpp/Download/Standard/Population/. (accessed June 15, 2021).

United States Census Bureau. "Current Population Survey Data Tools." https://www.census.gov/programs-surveys/cps/data/data-tools.html. (accessed June 15, 2021).

Williams, Aaron; Emamdjomeh, Armand. "America is more diverse than ever – but still segregated." *The Washington Post*. https://www.washingtonpost.com/graphics/2018/national/segregation-us-cities/. (accessed June 15, 2021).

The National Museum of the American Indian. "Frequently Asked Questions." https://americanindian.si.edu/nk360/faq/did-you-know. (accessed June 15, 2021).

Jan, Tracy. "Redlining was banned 50 years ago. It's still hurting minorities today." *The Washington Post*. https://www.washingtonpost.com/news/wonk/wp/2018/03/28/redlining-was-banned-50-years-ago-its-still-hurting-minorities-today/. (accessed June 15, 2021).

Weldon Cooper Center for Public Service. "The Racial Dot Map." The University of Virginia. https://demographics.coopercenter.org/racial-dot-map. (accessed June 15, 2021).

"Mapping Inequality." https://demographics.coopercenter.org/racial-dot-map-access-and-use-policy

Frey, William H. "The US will become 'minority white' in 2045, Census projects." The Brookings Institution. https://www.brookings.edu/blog/the-avenue/2018/03/14/the-us-will-become-minority-white-in-2045-census-projects/. (accessed June 15, 2021).

About the Authors

Matt Felton-Koestler and Courtney Koestler live in Athens, Ohio, where they are faculty members in the Department of Teacher Education in the Patton College of Education at Ohio University. They like to spend time with their kid, Parker, and their cat, Bitsy, and spend time outdoors with their friends.

Photos by Ben Siegel, Ohio University Photographer

© 2022 Rourke Educational Media

All rights reserved. No part of this book may be reproduced or utilized in any form or by any means, electronic or mechanical including photocopying, recording, or by any information storage and retrieval system without permission in writing from the publisher.

www.rourkeeducationalmedia.com

PHOTO CREDITS: cover, page 1: franckreporter/ Getty Images; cover, page 1: traffic_analyzer/ Getty Images; page 4: Rawpixel/Getty Images; page 5: viavado/Getty Images; page 6: Rawpixel/Getty Images; page 7: Harvepino/ Getty Images; page 8: wildpixel/Getty Images; page 10: QUINN GLABICKI/REUTERS/ Newscom; page 11: Presidentman/ Wikipedia Commons; page 12: vm/Getty Images; page 14: DMEPhotography/ Getty Images; page 15: Oleg Elkov/ Getty Images; page 15: PeopleImages/ Getty Images; page 15: RyanJLane/Getty Images; page 15: florin1961/ Getty Images; page 16: SolStock/ Getty Images; page 17: nazar_ab/ Getty Images; page 18: Alessandro Biascioli/Getty Images; page 18: baona/ Getty Images; page 20: Ljupco Smokovski/ Shutterstock.com; page 22: Julesinski/ Getty Images; page 23: Jmonkeybusinessimages/ Getty Images; page 24: SolStock/Getty Images; page 26: Jupiterimages/Getty Images; page 26: benedek/Getty Images; page 26: Ingo370/ Shutterstock.com; page 26-27 jjwithers/Getty Images; page 27: halbergman/Getty Images; page 27: wellesenterprises/Getty Images; page 28: Phillip Harrington / Alamy Stock Photo; page 29: Monkey Business Images/ Shutterstock.com; page 29: Feverpitched/ Getty Images; page 29: SerrNovik/ Getty Images; page 30-31: ellisonphoto/ Getty Images; page 31: From The Washington Post. © 2018 The Washington Post. All rights reserved. Used under license.; page 32: AnthonyRosenberg/ Getty Images; page 33: Robert K. Nelson, LaDale Winling, Richard Marciano, Nathan Connolly, et al., "Mapping Inequality," American Panorama, ed.; page 33: Robert K. Nelson, LaDale Winling, Richard Marciano, Nathan Connolly, et al., "Mapping Inequality," American Panorama, ed.; page 33: Robert K. Nelson, LaDale Winling, Richard Marciano, Nathan Connolly, et al., "Mapping Inequality," American Panorama, ed.; page 34: Robert K. Nelson, LaDale Winling, Richard Marciano, Nathan Connolly, et al., "Mapping Inequality," American Panorama, ed.; page 34-35: Robert K. Nelson, LaDale Winling, Richard Marciano, Nathan Connolly, et al., "Mapping Inequality," American Panorama, ed.; page 35: Robert K. Nelson, LaDale Winling, Richard Marciano, Nathan Connolly, et al., "Mapping Inequality," American Panorama, ed.; page 36: SDI Productions/ Getty Images; page 37: peeterv/ Getty Images; page 38: fstop123/ Getty Images; page 39: Department of Housing and Urban Development (HUD.gov); page 39: Department of Housing and Urban Development (HUD.gov); page 40-41: photovs/ Getty Images; page 41: Leif Skoogfors / Contributor/ Getty Images; page 42: Sergei Nedelkin; page 43: ljubaphoto/ Getty Images; page 43: LeoPatrizi/ Getty Images; page 44: 4x6/ Getty Images

Library of Congress PCN Data

Communities Near and Far / Felton-Koestler, Koestler
(Data In Your World)
ISBN 9781-7-3165-175-4 (hard cover)
ISBN 9781-7-3165-220-1 (soft cover)
ISBN 9781-7-3165-190-7 (e-Book)
ISBN 9781-7-3165-205-8 (epub)
Library of Congress Control Number: 2021944575

Rourke Educational Media
Printed in the United States of America
04-1452413123

Edited by: **Cary Malaski**
Cover and interior design by: **J.J. Giddings**